EP 173 (1368); NP 1034 or 1037

1. **Fri. MARY, MOTHER OF GOD (Sol) 175**
   MP 175 (707); DP 1027; EP 178; NP 1037

2. Sat. Sts. Basil the Great and Gregory Nazianzen, Bb & Dd (Mem) 1060
   MP (1426 or 1435) (Ant) 770; DP 1022
   EP 207; NP 1034

3. **Sun. EPIPHANY (Sol) 211**
   MP 211 (707); DP 1027; EP 214; NP 1037

4. Mon. St. Elizabeth Ann Seton (Mem) 1061
   MP (1470) 792; DP 998; EP (1471) 798; NP 1041

5. Tue. St. John Neumann, B (Mem) 1062
   MP (1426) 802; DP 1003; EP (1430) 807; NP 1044

6. Wed. Wednesday after Epiphany or St. André Bessette, Rel **(New)** (5)
   MP (225) (1470) 812 Pr proper (6) or 1471; DP 1008
   EP (226) (1471) 818 Pr (6) or 1471; NP 1046

7. Thu. Thursday after Epiphany or St. Raymond of Penyafort, P (1063)
   MP (228) (1426) 824; DP 1012; EP (229) (1430) 830; NP 1049

8. Fri. Friday after Epiphany
   MP (231) 835; DP 1017; EP (233) 840; NP 1052

9. Sat. Saturday after Epiphany
   MP (235) 845; DP 1022; EP 207 (237); NP 1034

10. **Sun. BAPTISM OF THE LORD (F) 239**
    MP (239) 707; DP 994; EP 242 (214); NP 1037

11. Mon. Monday of the 1st Week in Ordinary Time
MP 718; DP 998; EP 723; NP 1041

12. Tue. Tuesday of the 1st Week in Ordinary Time
MP 728; DP 1003; EP 734; NP 1044

13. Wed. Weekday or St. Hilary, B & D (1063)
MP (1426 or 1435) 738; DP 1008; EP (1430 or 1436) 743; NP 1046

14. Thu. Thursday of the 1st Week in Ordinary Time
MP 748; DP 1012; EP 754; NP 1049

15. Fri. Friday of the 1st Week in Ordinary Time
MP 759; DP 1017; EP 765; NP 1052

16. Sat. Weekday or BVM on Saturday (1383)
MP (1383) 770; DP 1022; EP (246) 775; NP 1034

17. **Sun. SECOND SUNDAY IN ORDINARY TIME 246**
MP 780; DP 994; EP 786; NP 1037

18. Mon. Monday of the 2nd Week in Ordinary Time
MP 792; DP 998; EP 798; NP 1041

19. Tue. Tuesday of the 2nd Week in Ordinary Time
MP 802; DP 1003; EP 807; NP 1044

20. Wed. Weekday or St. Fabian, Po & M, or St. Sebastian, M (1065)
MP (1414 or 1426) 812; DP 1008
EP (1417 or 1430) 818; NP 1046

21. Thu. St. Agnes, V & M (Mem) 1065
MP 1066 (707); DP 1012; EP 1067 (1418); NP 1049

Saint Joseph

GUIDE

FOR

Christian Prayer

(The Liturgy of the Hours)

For use with Edition No. 407

2021

No. 407/G

CATHOLIC BOOK PUBLISHING CORP.
New Jersey
catholicbookpublishing.com

The purpose of this handy GUIDE is to facilitate use of CHRISTIAN PRAYER, the one-volume **Liturgy of the Hours**, by providing clear, accurate references for each day of the year—always in accord with the principles on which this particular Breviary was compiled. These principles are enunciated on pages 34-37 of the volume and the use of this GUIDE is dependent upon a thorough understanding of these directives. Whenever a Saint is celebrated as a Memorial, the numbers in parentheses refer to the page in the Common that is to be used; the numbers without parentheses refer to the page in the Psalter that is to be used. (See p. 37 under Memorials.)

The designation **(New)** indicates that the Saint in question is found in the revised **SUPPLEMENT of the Liturgy of the Hours** (No. 705/04) published in 1992. **(No SUPPLEMENT** has been approved for publication since that time.). The designation *(New)* in lightface italics indicates that the Saint in question must be taken from the pertinent Common.

For those who will use the Edition with Music and the Office of Readings, the pertinent information is supplied on a separate line within brackets at the end of each entry.

LIST OF ABBREVIATIONS

Ab — Abbot
Ant — Antiphon
Ap — Apostle
B, Bb — Bishop(s)
Bl. — Blessed
BVM — Blessed Virgin Mary
Comp(s) — Companion(s)
D, Dd — Doctor(s)
De — Deacon
Ded — Dedication of Church
DP — Daytime Prayer
EP — Evening Prayer
F — Feast
f — following page(s)
M, Mm — Martyr(s)

Mem — Memorial (Obligatory)
Miss — Missionaries
MP — Morning Prayer
NP — Night Prayer
OOR — Office of Readings
P, Pp — Priest(s)
Po — Pope
Pr — Prayer
Rd — Reading(s)
Rel — Religious
Sol — Solemnity
St., Sts. — Saint(s)
TD — Te Deum
V — Virgin

(407/G)

22. Fri. Day of Prayer for the Legal Protection of Unborn Children
MP 835; DP 1017; EP 840; NP 1052

23. Sat. Weekday or St. Vincent, De & M (1068) **[transferred from 1/22]** or St.
Marianne Cope, V *(New)* (1441 or 1472) or BVM on Saturday (1383)
MP (1414) (1441 or 1472) (1383) 845; DP 1022
EP 851 (247); NP 1034

24. **Sun. THIRD SUNDAY IN ORDINARY TIME 247**
MP 856; DP 994; EP 861; NP 1037

25. Mon. CONVERSION OF ST. PAUL, AP (F) 1069
MP 1069 (707); DP 998; EP 1071 (1394); NP 1041

26. Tue. Sts. Timothy and Titus, Bb (Mem) 1073
MP (1426) (Ant) 877; DP 1003
EP (1430) (Ant) 882; NP 1044

27. Wed. Weekday or St. Angela Merici, V (1074)
MP (1441 or 1473) 886; DP 1008
EP (1444 or 1473) 892; NP 1046

28. Thu. St. Thomas Aquinas, P & D (Mem) 1075
MP (1435) (Ant) 897; DP 1012; EP (1436) (Ant) 901; NP 1049

29. Fri. Friday of the 3rd Week in Ordinary Time
MP 906; DP 1017; EP 911; NP 1052

30. Sat. Weekday or BVM on Saturday (1383)
MP (1383) 916; DP 1022; EP 921 (248); NP 1034

31. **Sun. FOURTH SUNDAY IN ORDINARY TIME 248**
MP 925; DP 994; EP 931; NP 1037

FEBRUARY

1. Mon. Monday of the 4th Week in Ordinary Time
   MP 937; DP 998; EP 942; NP 1041

2. Tue. PRESENTATION OF THE LORD (F) 1081
   MP 1081 (707); DP 1003; EP 1082; NP 1044

3. Wed. Weekday or St. Blase, B & M (1086) or St. Ansgar, B (1087)
   MP (1414 or 1426) 958; DP 1008
   EP (1417 or 1430) 963; NP 1046

4. Thu. Thursday of the 4th Week in Ordinary Time
   MP 968; DP 1012; EP 973; NP 1049

5. Fri. St. Agatha, V & M (Mem) 1087
   MP (1414 or 1441) (Ant) 978; DP 1017
   EP (1417 or 1444) (Ant) 984; NP 1052

6. Sat. St. Paul Miki and Comps, Mm (Mem) 1088
   MP (1402) (Ant) 988; DP 1022; EP 701 (249); NP 1034

7. Sun. **FIFTH SUNDAY IN ORDINARY TIME 249**
   MP 706; DP 994; EP 712; NP 1037

8. Mon. Weekday or St. Jerome Emiliani (1089) or St. Josephine Bakhita, V
   (New) (1441)
   MP (1473) (1441) (Ant) 718; DP 998; EP (1473) (1444) (Ant) 723; NP 1041

9. Tue. Tuesday of the 5th Week in Ordinary Time
   MP 728; DP 1003; EP 734; NP 1044

10. Wed. St. Scholastica, V (Mem) 1090
    MP (1441) (Ant) 738; DP 1008; EP (1444) (Ant) 743; NP 1046

11. Thu. Weekday or Our Lady of Lourdes (1091)
MP (1372) (Ant) 748; DP 1012; EP (1378) (Ant) 754; NP 1049

12. Fri. Friday of the 5th Week in Ordinary Time
MP 759; DP 1017; EP 765; NP 1052

13. Sat. Weekday or BVM on Saturday (1383)
MP (1383) 770; DP 1022; EP (250) 775; NP 1034

14. **Sun. SIXTH SUNDAY IN ORDINARY TIME 250**
MP 780; DP 994; EP 786; NP 1037

15. Mon. Monday of the 6th Week in Ordinary Time
MP 792; DP 998; EP 798; NP 1041

16. Tue. Tuesday of the 6th Week in Ordinary Time
MP 802; DP 1003; EP 807; NP 1044

17. Wed. ASH WEDNESDAY 255
MP (255) 906 or 958; DP 1008; EP (256) 963; NP 1046

18. Thu. Thursday after Ash Wednesday
MP (258) 968; DP 1012; EP (259) 973; NP 1049

19. Fri. Friday after Ash Wednesday
MP (261) 978; DP 1017; EP (262) 984; NP 1052

20. Sat. Saturday after Ash Wednesday
MP (264) 988; DP 1022; EP (266) 701; NP 1034

21. **Sun. FIRST SUNDAY OF LENT 268**
MP (268) 707; DP 994; EP (270) 712; NP 1037

22. Mon. CHAIR OF ST. PETER, AP (F) 1095
     MP 1095 (707); DP 998; EP 1097 (1394); NP 1041

23. Tue. Tuesday of the 1st Week of Lent
     MP (275) 728 (St. Polycarp, B & M 1100); DP 1003
     EP (276) 734 (St. Polycarp, B & M 1100); NP 1044

24. Wed. Wednesday of the 1st Week of Lent
     MP (278) 738; DP 1008; EP (280) 743; NP 1046

25. Thu. Thursday of the 1st Week of Lent
     MP (281) 748; DP 1012; EP (283) 754; NP 1049

26. Fri. Friday of the 1st Week of Lent
     MP (285) 759; DP 1017; EP (286) 765; NP 1052

27. Sat. Saturday of the 1st Week of Lent
     MP (288) 770; DP 1022; EP (290) 775; NP 1034

28. **Sun. SECOND SUNDAY OF LENT 292**
     MP (292) 780; DP 994; EP (294) 786; NP 1037

MARCH

1. Mon. Monday of the 2nd Week of Lent
    MP (296) 792; DP 998; EP (297) 798; NP 1041

2. Tue. Tuesday of the 2nd Week of Lent
    MP (299) 802; DP 1003; EP (301) 807; NP 1044

3. Wed. Wednesday of the 2nd Week of Lent
    MP (302) 812 (St. Katharine Drexel, V [**New** (7) or 1442]); DP 1008
    EP (304) 818 (St. Katharine Drexel, V [(7) or 1442]); NP 1046

4. Thu. Thursday of the 2nd Week of Lent
    MP (306) 824 (St. Casimir 1101); DP 1012
    EP (307) 830 (St. Casimir 1101); NP 1049

5. Fri. Friday of the 2nd Week of Lent
    MP (309) 835; DP 1017; EP (310) 840; NP 1052

6. Sat. Saturday of the 2nd Week of Lent
    MP (312) 845; DP 1022; EP (314) 851; NP 1034

7. Sun. **THIRD SUNDAY OF LENT 316**
    MP (316) 856; DP 994; EP (318) 861; NP 1037

8. Mon. Monday of the 3rd Week of Lent
    MP (320) 867 (St. John of God, Rel 1103); DP 998
    EP (322) 872 (St. John of God, Rel 1103); NP 1041

9. Tue. Tuesday of the 3rd Week of Lent
    MP (323) 877 (St. Frances of Rome, Rel 1104); DP 1003
    EP (324) 882 (St. Frances of Rome, Rel 1104); NP 1044

10. Wed. Wednesday of the 3rd Week of Lent
    MP (326) 886; DP 1008; EP (328) 892; NP 1046

11. Thu. Thursday of the 3rd Week of Lent
    MP (329) 897; DP 1012; EP (331) 901; NP 1049

12. Fri. Friday of the 3rd Week of Lent
    MP (332) 906; DP 1017; EP (334) 911; NP 1052

13. Sat. Saturday of the 3rd Week of Lent
    MP (335) 916; DP 1022; EP (338) 921; NP 1034

14. Sun. **FOURTH SUNDAY OF LENT 340**
    MP (340) 926; DP 994; EP (342) 931; NP 1037

15. Mon. Monday of the 4th Week of Lent
    MP (344) 937; DP 998; EP (346) 942; NP 1041

16. Tue. Tuesday of the 4th Week of Lent
    MP (347) 947; DP 1003; EP (349) 953; NP 1044

17. Wed. Wednesday of the 4th Week of Lent
    MP (351) 958 (St. Patrick, B 1105); DP 1008
    EP (352) 963 (St. Patrick, B 1105); NP 1046

18. Thu. Thursday of the 4th Week of Lent
    MP (354) 968 (St. Cyril of Jerusalem, B & D 1106); DP 1012
    EP 1107 (1448); NP 1034

19. Fri. ST. JOSEPH, HUSBAND OF MARY (Sol) 1109
    MP 1109 (707); DP 1027; EP 1111; NP 1037

20. Sat. Saturday of the 4th Week of Lent
    MP (360) 988; DP 1022; EP (362) 701; NP 1034

21. **Sun. FIFTH SUNDAY OF LENT 364**
    MP (364) 707; DP 994; EP (366) 712; NP 1037

22. Mon. Monday of the 5th Week of Lent
    MP (368) 718; DP 998; EP (369) 723; NP 1041

23. Tue. Tuesday of the 5th Week of Lent
    MP (371) 728 (St. Toribius de Mogrovejo, B 1113); DP 1003
    EP (372) 734 (St. Toribius de Mogrovejo, B 1113); NP 1044

24. Wed. Wednesday of the 5th Week of Lent
    MP (374) 738; DP 1008; EP 1114; NP 1034

25. Thu. ANNUNCIATION OF THE LORD (Sol) 1118
    MP 1118 (707); DP 1027; EP 1120; NP 1037

26.   Fri. Friday of the 5th Week of Lent
MP (380) 759; DP 1017; EP (382) 765; NP 1052

27.   Sat. Saturday of the 5th Week of Lent
MP (383) 770; DP 1022; EP (386) 775; NP 1034

28.   **Sun. PASSION SUNDAY (PALM SUNDAY) 388**
MP (388) 780; DP 994; EP (390) 786; NP 1037

29.   Mon. MONDAY OF HOLY WEEK
MP (393) 792; DP 998; EP (395) 798; NP 1041

30.   Tue. TUESDAY OF HOLY WEEK
MP (397) 802; DP 1003; EP (398) 807; NP 1044

31.   Wed. WEDNESDAY OF HOLY WEEK
MP (400) 812; DP 1008; EP (402) 819; NP 1046

APRIL

1.   Thu. HOLY THURSDAY 404
MP 824 (404); DP 1012; EP 830 (406); NP 1037

2.   Fri. GOOD FRIDAY 408
MP 408; DP 1017; EP 413; NP 1037

3.   Sat. HOLY SATURDAY 417
MP 417; DP 1022; EP 422; NP 1037

4.   **Sun. EASTER SUNDAY 427**
MP 427 (707); DP 994; EP 429; NP 1037

5.   Mon. MONDAY WITHIN THE OCTAVE OF EASTER
MP 427 & 434; DP 998; EP 429 & 435; NP 1034 or 1037

6. Tue. TUESDAY WITHIN THE OCTAVE OF EASTER
    MP 427 & 437; DP 1003; EP 429 & 438; NP 1034 & 1037

7. Wed. WEDNESDAY WITHIN THE OCTAVE OF EASTER
    MP 427 & 440; DP 1008; EP 429 & 441; NP 1034 & 1037

8. Thu. THURSDAY WITHIN THE OCTAVE OF EASTER
    MP 427 & 443; DP 1012; EP 429 & 444; NP 1034 or 1037

9. Fri. FRIDAY WITHIN THE OCTAVE OF EASTER
    MP 427 & 446; DP 1017; EP 429 & 447; NP 1034 or 1037

10. Sat. SATURDAY WITHIN THE OCTAVE OF EASTER
    MP 427 & 449; DP 1022; EP 429 & 451; NP 1034 or 1037

11. Sun. **SECOND SUNDAY OF EASTER 453**
    MP 427 & 453; DP 994; EP 429 & 455; NP 1037

12. Mon. Monday of the 2nd Week of Easter
    MP (457) 792; DP 998; EP (458) 798; NP 1041

13. Tue. Easter Weekday or St. Martin I, Po & M (1129)
    MP (1414 or 1426) (460) 802; DP 1003
    EP (1417 or 1430) (461) 807; NP 1044

14. Wed. Wednesday of the 2nd Week of Easter
    MP (463) 812; DP 1008; EP (464) 818; NP 1046

15. Thu. Thursday of the 2nd Week of Easter
    MP (466) 824; DP 1012; EP (467) 830; NP 1049

16. Fri. Friday of the 2nd Week of Easter
    MP (468) 835; DP 1017; EP (470) 840; NP 1052

17.   Sat. Saturday of the 2nd Week of Easter
MP (471) 845; DP 1022; EP (474) 851; NP 1034

18.   **Sun. THIRD SUNDAY OF EASTER 476**
MP (476) 856; DP 994; EP (478) 861; NP 1037

19.   Mon. Monday of the 3rd Week of Easter
MP (480) 867; DP 998; EP (481) 872; NP 1041

20.   Tue. Tuesday of the 3rd Week of Easter
MP (483) 877; DP 1003; EP (484) 882; NP 1044

21.   Wed. Easter Weekday or St. Anselm, B & D (1130)
MP (1426 or 1435) (486) 886; DP 1008
EP (1430 or 1436) (487) 892; NP 1046

22.   Thu. Thursday of the 3rd Week of Easter
MP (489) 897; DP 1012; EP (490) 901; NP 1049

23.   Fri. Easter Weekday or St. George, M (1130) or St. Adalbert, B & M *(New)*
      (1426 or 1414)
MP (1414) (1426 or 1414) (491) 906; DP 1017
EP (1417) (1430 or 1417) (493) 911; NP 1052

24.   Sat. Easter Weekday or St. Fidelis of Sigmaringen, P & M (1131)
MP (1414 or 1426) (494) 916; DP 1022
EP (496) 921; NP 1034

25.   **Sun. FOURTH SUNDAY OF EASTER 498**
MP (498) 926; DP 994; EP (500) 931; NP 1037

26.   Mon. Monday of the 4th Week of Easter
MP (502) 937; DP 998; EP (503) 942; NP 1041

27. Tue. Tuesday of the 4th Week of Easter
     MP (505) 947; DP 1003; EP (506) 953; NP 1044

28. Wed. Easter Weekday or St. Peter Chanel, P & M (1136) or St. Louis
        Grignion de Montfort, P *(New)* (1426 or 1470)
     MP (1414) (1426 or 1470) (508) 958; DP 1008
     EP (1417) (1430 or 1471) (509) 963; NP 1046

29. Thu. St. Catherine of Siena, V & D (Mem) 1136
     MP (1441) (Ant) 968; DP 1012; EP (1444) (Ant) 973; NP 1049

30. Fri. Easter Weekday or St. Pius V, Po (1137)
     MP (1426) (514) 978; DP 1017; EP (1430) (515) 984; NP 1052

MAY

1. Sat. Easter Weekday or St. Joseph the Worker (1139)
    MP (1139) (517) 988; DP 1022; EP (519) 701; NP 1034

2. **Sun. FIFTH SUNDAY OF EASTER 521**
    MP (521) 707; DP 994; EP (523) 712; NP 1037

3. Mon. STS. PHILIP AND JAMES, AP (F) 1143
    MP 1143 (707); DP 998; EP 1145 (1394); NP 1041

4. Tue. Tuesday of the 5th Week of Easter
    MP (528) 728; DP 1003; EP (529) 734; NP 1044

5. Wed. Wednesday of the 5th Week of Easter
    MP (531) 738; DP 1008; EP (532) 743; NP 1046

6. Thu. Thursday of the 5th Week of Easter
    MP (533) 748; DP 1012; EP (535) 754; NP 1049

7. Fri. Friday of the 5th Week of Easter
MP (536) 759; DP 1017; EP (538) 765; NP 1052

8. Sat. Saturday of the 5th Week of Easter
MP (539) 770; DP 1022; EP (541) 775; NP 1034

9. **Sun. SIXTH SUNDAY OF EASTER 543**
MP (543) 780; DP 994; EP (545) 786; NP 1037

10. Mon. Easter Weekday or St. Damien de Veuster of Molokai, P *(New)* (1426)
MP (1426) (547) 792; DP 998; EP (1430) (548) 798; NP 1041

11. Tue. Tuesday of the 6th Week of Easter
MP (549) 802; DP 1003; EP (551) 807; NP 1044

12. Wed. Easter Weekday or Sts. Nereus and Achilleus, Mm (1147) or St. Pancras, M (1148)
MP (1402) (1414) (552) 812; DP 1008; EP 559; NP 1034

13. **Thu. ASCENSION (Sol) 562**
MP (563) 707; DP 1027; EP 565; NP 1037

14. Fri. ST. MATTHIAS, AP (F) 1148
MP 1392 (Ant) (707); DP 1017; EP 1394 (Ant); NP 1052

15. Sat. Easter Weekday or St. Isidore (1149)
MP (1452) (574) 845; DP 1022; EP (577) 851; NP 1034

16. **Sun. SEVENTH SUNDAY OF EASTER 579**
MP (579) 856; DP 994; EP (581) 862; NP 1037

WHERE THE ASCENSION IS NOT TO BE OBSERVED AS A HOLYDAY OF OBLIGATION, IT IS ASSIGNED TO THE SEVENTH SUNDAY OF EASTER. **The specified rubrics below are to be followed until Monday of the 7th Week of Easter.**

12. Wed. Easter Weekday or Sts. Nereus and Achilleus, Mm (1147) or
       St. Pancras, M (1148)
    MP (1402) (1414) (552) 812; DP 1008
    EP (1405) (1417) (554) 818; NP 1046

13. Thu. Easter Weekday or Our Lady of Fatima *(New)* Common of the
       Blessed Virgin Mary (1372)
    MP (1372) (556) 824; DP 1012; EP (1378) (557) 830; NP 1049

14. Fri. ST. MATTHIAS, AP (F) 1148
    MP 1392 (Ant) (707); DP 1017; EP 1394 (Ant); NP 1052

15. Sat. Easter Weekday or St. Isidore (1149)
    MP (1452) (574) 845; DP 1022; EP 559; NP 1034

16. **Sun. ASCENSION (Sol) 562**
    MP (563) 707; DP 1027; EP 565; NP 1037

17. Mon. Monday of the 7th Week of Easter
    MP (583) 867; DP 998; EP (584) 872; NP 1041

18. Tue. Easter Weekday or St. John I, Po & M (1150)
    MP (1414 or 1426) (586) 877; DP 1003
    EP (1417 or 1430) (587) 882; NP 1044

19. Wed. Wednesday of the 7th Week of Easter
    MP (588) 886; DP 1008; EP (590) 892; NP 1046

20. Thu. Easter Weekday or St. Bernardine of Siena, P (1150)
    MP (1426 or 1470) (591) 897; DP 1012
    EP (1430 or 1471) (592) 901; NP 1049

21. Fri. Easter Weekday or St. Christopher Magallanes, P, and Comps, Mm
       (New) (1402 or 1426)
    MP (1402 or 1426) (594) 906; DP 1017
    EP (1405 or 1430) (595) 911; NP 1052

22. Sat. Weekday or St. Rita of Cascia, Rel *(New)* (1462 & 1470)
     MP (1462 or 1470) (597) 916; DP 1022; EP 599; NP 1034

23. **Sun. PENTECOST (Sol) 603**
     MP 603 (707); DP 1027; EP 605; NP 1037

24. Mon. The Blessed Virgin Mary, Mother of the Church (Mem) *(New)*
         Common of the Blessed Virgin Mary (1372)
     MP (1372) 937; DP 998; EP (1378) 942; NP 1041

25. Tue. Weekday or Venerable Bede, P & D (1151) or St. Gregory VII, Po
         (1152) or St. Mary Magdalene de Pazzi, V (1152)
     MP (1435 or 1470) (1426) (1441 or 1470) 947; DP 1003
     EP (1436 or 1471) (1430) (1444 or 1471) 953; NP 1044

26. Wed. St. Philip Neri, P (Mem) 1153
     MP (1426 or 1470) 958; DP 1008; EP (1430 or 1471) 963; NP 1046

27. Thu. Weekday or St. Augustine of Canterbury, B (1154)
     MP (1426) 968; DP 1012; EP (1430) 973; NP 1049

28. Fri. Friday of the 8th Week in Ordinary Time
     MP 978; DP 1017; EP 984; NP 1052

29. Sat. Weekday or St. Paul VI, Po *(New)* (1426) or BVM on Saturday (1383)
     MP (1426) (1383) 988; DP 1022; EP 641; NP 1034

30. **Sun. TRINITY SUNDAY (Sol) 645**
     MP 645 (707); DP 1027; EP 648; NP 1037

31. Mon. VISITATION OF MARY (F) 1154
     MP 1154 (707); DP 998; EP 1156 (1378); NP 1041

JUNE

1. Tue. St. Justin, M (Mem) 1160
    MP (1414) (Ant) 728; DP 1003; EP (1417) (Ant) 734; NP 1044

2. Wed. Weekday or Sts. Marcellinus and Peter, Mm (1161)
    MP (1402) 738; DP 1008; EP (1405) 743; NP 1046

3. Thu. Sts. Charles Lwanga and Comps, Mm (Mem) 1161
    MP (1402) 748; DP 1012; EP (1405) 754; NP 1049

4. Fri. Friday of the 9th Week in Ordinary Time
    MP 759; DP 1017; EP 765; NP 1052

5. Sat. St. Boniface, B & M (Mem) 1162
    MP (1414 or 1426) 770; DP 1022; EP 652; NP 1034

6. **Sun. CORPUS CHRISTI (Sol) 656**
    MP 656 (707); DP 1027; EP 658; NP 1037

7. Mon. Monday of the 10th Week in Ordinary Time
    MP 792; DP 998; EP 798; NP 1041

8. Tue. Tuesday of the 10th Week in Ordinary Time
    MP 802; DP 1003; EP 807; NP 1044

9. Wed. Weekday or St. Ephrem, De & D (1164)
    MP (1435) 812; DP 1008; EP (1436) 818; NP 1046

10. Thu. Thursday of the 10th Week in Ordinary Time
    MP 824; DP 1012; EP 663; NP 1034

11. Fri. SACRED HEART (Sol) 667
    MP 667 (707); DP 1027; EP 669; NP 1037

12. Sat. Immaculate Heart of Mary (1159)
     MP (1372) (Ant) 845; DP 1022; EP 851 (615); NP 1034

13. **Sun. ELEVENTH SUNDAY IN ORDINARY TIME 615**
     MP 856; DP 994; EP 861; NP 1037

14. Mon. Monday of the 11th Week in Ordinary Time
     MP 867; DP 998; EP 872; NP 1041

15. Tue. Tuesday of the 11th Week in Ordinary Time
     MP 877; DP 1003; EP 882; NP 1044

16. Wed. Wednesday of the 11th Week in Ordinary Time
     MP 886; DP 1008; EP 892; NP 1046

17. Thu. Thursday of the 11th Week in Ordinary Time
     MP 897; DP 1012; EP 901; NP 1049

18. Fri. Friday of the 11th Week in Ordinary Time
     MP 906; DP 1017; EP 911; NP 1052

19. Sat. Weekday or St. Romuald, Ab (1169) or BVM on Saturday (1383)
     MP (1470) (1383) 916; DP 1022; EP 921 (616); NP 1034

20. **Sun. TWELFTH SUNDAY IN ORDINARY TIME 616**
     MP 925; DP 994; EP 931; NP 1037

21. Mon. St. Aloysius Gonzaga, Rel (Mem) 1169
     MP (1470) 937; DP 998; EP (1471) 942; NP 1041

22. Tue. Weekday or St. Paulinus of Nola, B (1170) or Sts. John Fisher, B & M,
       and Thomas More, M (1171)
     MP (1426) (1402) 947; DP 1003; EP (1430) (1405) 953; NP 1044

23. Wed. Wednesday of the 12th Week in Ordinary Time
    MP 958; DP 1008; EP 1172 (1448); NP 1034

24. Thu. BIRTH OF ST. JOHN THE BAPTIST (Sol) 1174
    MP 1174 (707); DP 1027
    EP 1176 (1456); NP 1037

25. Fri. Friday of the 12th Week in Ordinary Time
    MP 978; DP 1017; EP 984; NP 1052

26. Sat. Weekday or BVM on Saturday (1383)
    MP (1383) 988; DP 1022; EP 701 (617); NP 1034

27. **Sun. THIRTEENTH SUNDAY IN ORDINARY TIME 617**
    MP 706; DP 994; EP 712; NP 1037

28. Mon. St. Irenaeus, B & M (Mem) 1178
    MP (1414 or 1426) (Ant) 718; DP 998
    EP 1179 (1389); NP 1034

29. Tue. STS. PETER AND PAUL, AP (Sol) 1181
    MP 1181 (707); DP 1027; EP 1183 (1394); NP 1037

30. Wed. Weekday or First Martyrs of the Church of Rome (1185)
    MP (1402) (Ant) 738; DP 1008; EP (1405) (Ant) 743; NP 1046

JULY

1. Thu. Weekday or St. Junipero Serra, P **(New)** (8)
   MP (1426 or 1470) 748, Pr (8) or 1429; DP 1012
   EP (1430 or 1471) 754, Pr (8) or 1429; NP 1049

2. Fri. Friday of the 13th Week in Ordinary Time
   MP 759; DP 1017; EP 765; NP 1052

3. Sat. ST. THOMAS, AP (F) 1186
    MP 1187 (707); DP 1022; EP 775 (618); NP 1034

4. Sun. **FOURTEENTH SUNDAY IN ORDINARY TIME 618**
    MP 780; DP 994; EP 786; NP 1037

5. Mon. Weekday or St. Anthony Zaccaria, P (1190) or St. Elizabeth of
        Portugal (1189) **[transferred from 7/4]**
    MP (1426 or 1473 or 1470) (1472) 792; DP 998
    EP (1430 or 1473 or 1471) (1472) 798; NP 1041

6. Tue. Weekday or St. Maria Goretti, V & M (1190)
    MP (1414 or 1441) 802; DP 1003; EP (1417 or 1444) 807; NP 1044

7. Wed. Wednesday of the 14th Week in Ordinary Time
    MP 812; DP 1008; EP 818; NP 1046

8. Thu. Thursday of the 14th Week in Ordinary Time
    MP 824; DP 1012; EP 830; NP 1049

9. Fri. Weekday or St. Augustine Zhao Rong, P, and Comps, Mm *(New)*
        (1402 or 1426)
    MP 835; DP 1017; EP 840; NP 1052

10. Sat. Weekday or BVM on Saturday (1383)
    MP (1383) 845; DP 1022; EP 851 (619); NP 1034

11. Sun. **FIFTEENTH SUNDAY IN ORDINARY TIME 619**
    MP 856; DP 994; EP 861; NP 1037

12. Mon. Monday of the 15th Week in Ordinary Time
    MP 867; DP 998; EP 872; NP 1041

13. Tue. Weekday or St. Henry (1192)
    MP (1452) 877; DP 1003; EP (1455) 882; NP 1044

14. Wed. St. Kateri Tekakwitha, V (Mem) **(New)** (9)
    MP (1441) 886, Pr proper (9) or 1443; DP 1008
    EP (1444) 892, Pr proper (9) or 1447; NP 1046

15. Thu. St. Bonaventure, B & D (Mem) 1193
    MP (1426 or 1435) 897; DP 1012
    EP (1430 or 1436) 901; NP 1049

16. Fri. Weekday or Our Lady of Mount Carmel (1194)
    MP (1372) (Ant) 906; DP 1017; EP (1378) (Ant) 911; NP 1052

17. Sat. Weekday or BVM on Saturday (1383)
    MP (1383) 916; DP 1022; EP (620) 921; NP 1034

18. **Sun. SIXTEENTH SUNDAY IN ORDINARY TIME 620**
    MP 925; DP 994; EP 931; NP 1037

19. Mon. Monday of the 16th Week in Ordinary Time
    MP 937; DP 998; EP 942; NP 1041

20. Tue. Weekday or St. Apollinaris, B & M *(New)* (1414 or 1426)
    MP (1414 or 1426) 947; DP 1003; EP (1417 or 1430) 953; NP 1044

21. Wed. Weekday or St. Lawrence of Brindisi, P & D (1195)
    MP (1426 or 1435) 958; DP 1008
    EP (1430 or 1436) 963; NP 1046

22. Thu. ST. MARY MAGDALENE (F) 1195
    MP 1196 (707); DP 1012; EP 1197 (1466); NP 1049

23. Fri. Weekday or St. Bridget, Rel (1198)
    MP (1470) 978; DP 1017; EP (1471) 984; NP 1052

24. Sat. Weekday or St. Sharbel Makhlūf, P *(New)* (1426) or BVM on
    Saturday (1383)
    MP (1426) (1383) 988; DP 1022; EP (621) 701; NP 1034

25.　**Sun. SEVENTEENTH SUNDAY IN ORDINARY TIME 621**
　　　MP 706; DP 994; EP 712; NP 1037

26.　Mon. Sts. Joachim and Ann, Parents of Mary (Mem) 1201
　　　MP 1202 (718); DP 998; EP 1203 (723); NP 1041

27.　Tue. Tuesday of the 17th Week in Ordinary Time
　　　MP 728; DP 1003; EP 734; NP 1044

28.　Wed. Wednesday of the 17th Week in Ordinary Time
　　　MP 738; DP 1008; EP 743; NP 1046

29.　Thu. St. Martha (Mem) 1203
　　　MP (1463) (Ant) 748; DP 1012; EP (1466) (Ant) 754; NP 1049

30.　Fri. Weekday or St. Peter Chrysologus, B & D (1204)
　　　MP (1426 or 1435) 759; DP 1017; EP (1430 or 1436) 765; NP 1052

31.　Sat. St. Ignatius of Loyola, P (Mem) 1205
　　　MP (1426 or 1470) (Ant) 770; DP 1022; EP (622) 775; NP 1034

AUGUST

1.　**Sun. EIGHTEENTH SUNDAY IN ORDINARY TIME 622**
　　　MP 780; DP 994; EP 786; NP 1037

2.　Mon. Weekday or St. Eusebius of Vercelli, B (1207) or St. Peter Julian
　　　　Eymard, P (New) (1426 or 1470)
　　　MP (1426) (1470) 792; DP 998
　　　EP (1430) (1471) 798; NP 1041

3. Tue. Tuesday of the 18th Week in Ordinary Time
    MP 802; DP 1003; EP 807; NP 1044

4. Wed. St. John Vianney, P (Mem) 1208
    MP (1426) 812; DP 1008; EP (1430) 818; NP 1046

5. Thu. Weekday or Dedication of St. Mary Major (1208)
    MP (1372) (Ant) 824; DP 1012; EP (1378) (Ant) 830; NP 1049

6. Fri. TRANSFIGURATION OF OUR LORD (F) 1213
    MP 1213 (707); DP 1017; EP 1215; NP 1052

7. Sat. Weekday or St. Sixtus II, Po & M, and Comps, Mm (1219) or St.
    Cajetan, P (1220) or BVM on Saturday (1383)
    MP (1426 or 1470) (1402) (1383) 845; DP 1022
    EP 851 (623); NP 1034

8. **Sun. NINETEENTH SUNDAY IN ORDINARY TIME 623**
    MP 856; DP 994; EP 861; NP 1037

9. Mon. Weekday or St. Teresa Benedicta of the Cross, V & M (Edith
    Stein) (New) (1414 or 1441)
    MP (1414 or 1441) 867; DP 998; EP (1417 or 1444) 872; NP 1041

10. Tue. ST. LAWRENCE, De & M (F) 1221
    MP 1221 (707); DP 1003; EP 1223 (1417); NP 1044

11. Wed. St. Clare, V (Mem) 1224
    MP (1441 or 1470) 886; DP 1008; EP (1444 or 1471) 892; NP 1046

12. Thu. Weekday or St. Jane Frances de Chantal, Rel (1340) or **(New)** (14)
    [transferred from 8/18]
    MP (1470) 897; DP 1012; EP (1471) 901; NP 1049

13. Fri. Weekday or Sts. Pontian, Po & M, and Hippolytus, P & M (1224)
     MP (1402 or 1426) 906; DP 1017; EP (1405 or 1430) 911; NP 1052

14. Sat. St. Maximilian Kolbe, P & M (Mem) **(New)** (10)
     MP (1414 or 1426) (Ant & Pr proper [14]) 916; DP 1022
     EP 1225 (1368); NP 1034

15. **Sun. ASSUMPTION (Sol) 1227**
     MP 1227 (707); DP 1027; EP 1229 (1378); NP 1037

16. Mon. Weekday or St. Stephen of Hungary (1231)
     MP (1452) 937; DP 998; EP (1455) 942; NP 1041

17. Tue. Tuesday of the 20th Week in Ordinary Time
     MP 947; DP 1003; EP 953; NP 1044

18. Wed. Wednesday of the 20th Week in Ordinary Time
     MP 958; DP 1008; EP 963; NP 1046

19. Thu. Weekday or St. John Eudes, P (1232)
     MP (1426 or 1470) 968; DP 1012; EP (1430 or 1471) 973; NP 1049

20. Fri. St. Bernard, Ab & D (Mem) 1232
     MP (1434 or 1470) (Ant) 978; DP 1017
     EP (1436 or 1471) (Ant) 984; NP 1052

21. Sat. St. Pius X, Po (Mem) 1233
     MP (1426) 988; DP 1022; EP 701 (626); NP 1034

22. **Sun. TWENTY-FIRST SUNDAY IN ORDINARY TIME 626**
     MP 706; DP 994; EP 712; NP 1037

23. Mon. Weekday or St. Rose of Lima, V (1235)
     MP (1441 or 1470) 718; DP 998; EP (1444 or 1471) 723; NP 1041

24. Tue. ST. BARTHOLOMEW, AP (F) 1236
     MP 1392 (707); DP 1003; EP 1394; NP 1044

25. Wed. Weekday or St. Louis (1236) or St. Joseph Calasanz, P (1237)
     MP (1452) (1473 or 1426) 738; DP 1008
     EP (1455) (1473 or 1430) 743; NP 1046

26. Thu. Thursday of the 21st Week in Ordinary Time
     MP 748; DP 1012; EP 754; NP 1049

27. Fri. St. Monica (Mem) 1238
     MP (1463) (Ant) 759; DP 1017; EP (1466) (Ant) 765; NP 1052

28. Sat. St. Augustine, B & D (Mem) 1239
     MP (1426 or 1435) (Ant) 770; DP 1022; EP (627) 775; NP 1034

29. **Sun. TWENTY-SECOND SUNDAY IN ORDINARY TIME 627**
     MP 780; DP 994; EP 786; NP 1037

30. Mon. Monday of the 22nd Week in Ordinary Time
     MP 792; DP 998; EP 798; NP 1041

31. Tue. Tuesday of the 22nd Week in Ordinary Time
     MP 802; DP 1003; EP 807; NP 1044

SEPTEMBER

1. Wed. Wednesday of the 22nd Week in Ordinary Time
    MP 812; DP 1008; EP 818; NP 1046

2. Thu. Thursday of the 22nd Week in Ordinary Time
    MP 824; DP 1012; EP 830; NP 1049

3. Fri. St. Gregory the Great, Po & D (Mem) 1244
    MP (1426 or 1435) (Ant) 835; DP 1017
    EP (1430 or 1436) (Ant) 840; NP 1052

4. Sat. Weekday or BVM on Saturday (1383)
    MP (1383) 845; DP 1022; EP (628) 851; NP 1034

5. Sun. **TWENTY-THIRD SUNDAY IN ORDINARY TIME 628**
    MP 856; DP 994; EP 861; NP 1037

6. Mon. Monday of the 23rd Week in Ordinary Time
    MP 867; DP 998; EP 872; NP 1041

7. Tue. Tuesday of the 23rd Week in Ordinary Time
    MP 877; DP 1003; EP 882; NP 1044

8. Wed. BIRTH OF MARY (F) 1245
    MP 1245 (707); DP 1008; EP 1247 (1378); NP 1046

9. Thu. St. Peter Claver, P (Mem) 1248
    MP (1426 or 1472) 897; DP 1012
    EP (1430 or 1472) 901; NP 1049

10. Fri. Friday of the 23rd Week in Ordinary Time
    MP 906; DP 1017; EP 911; NP 1052

11. Sat. Weekday or BVM on Saturday (1383)
    MP (1383) 916; DP 1022; EP (629) 921; NP 1034

12. Sun. **TWENTY-FOURTH SUNDAY IN ORDINARY TIME 629**
    MP 925; DP 994; EP 931; NP 1037

13. Mon. St. John Chrysostom, B & D (Mem) 1249
    MP (1426 or 1435) 937; DP 998
    EP (1430 or 1436) 942; NP 1041

14. Tue. TRIUMPH OF THE CROSS (F) 1254
     MP 1254 (707); DP 1003; EP 1256; NP 1044

15. Wed. Our Lady of Sorrows (Mem) 1260
     MP 1261 (707); DP 1008; EP 1262 (1378); NP 1046

16. Thu. Sts. Cornelius, Po & M, and Cyprian, B & M (Mem) 1263
     MP (1402 or 1426) (Ant) 968; DP 1012
     EP (1405 or 1430) (Ant) 973; NP 1049

17. Fri. Weekday or St. Robert Bellarmine, B & D (1265)
     MP (1426 or 1435) 978; DP 1017; EP (1430 or 1436) 984; NP 1052

18. Sat. Weekday or BVM on Saturday (1383)
     MP (1383) 988; DP 1022; EP (630) 701; NP 1034

19. **Sun. TWENTY-FIFTH SUNDAY IN ORDINARY TIME 630**
     MP 706; DP 994; EP 712; NP 1037

20. Mon. Sts. Andrew Kim Taegŏn, P & M, Paul Chŏng Hasang, and
         Comps, Mm (Mem) **(New)** (17)
     MP (1402) 718, Pr proper (21); DP 998; EP (1405) 723; NP 1041

21. Tue. ST. MATTHEW, AP & EVANGELIST (F) 1266
     MP 1392 (707) (Ant); DP 1003; EP 1394 (Ant); NP 1044

22. Wed. Wednesday of the 25th Week in Ordinary Time
     MP 738; DP 1008; EP 743; NP 1046

23. Thu. St. Pius of Pietrelcina, P (Mem) *(New)* (1426)
     MP (1426) 748; DP 1012; EP (1430) 754; NP 1049

24. Fri. Friday of the 25th Week in Ordinary Time
     MP 759; DP 1017; EP 765; NP 1052

25. Sat. Weekday or BVM on Saturday (1383)
     MP (1383) 770; DP 1022; EP (631) 775; NP 1034

26. Sun. **TWENTY-SIXTH SUNDAY IN ORDINARY TIME 632**
     MP 780; DP 994; EP 786; NP 1037

27. Mon. St. Vincent de Paul, P (Mem) 1267
     MP (1426 or 1472) (Ant) 792; DP 998
     EP (1430 or 1472) (Ant) 798; NP 1041

28. Tue. Weekday or St. Wenceslaus, M (1268) or St. Lawrence Ruiz and
         Comps, Mm **(New)** (21), Pr proper (24) or 1404
     MP (1414) (1402) 802; DP 1003; EP (1417) (1405) 807; NP 1044

29. Wed. STS. MICHAEL, GABRIEL AND RAPHAEL, ARCHANGELS (F) 1269
     MP 1269 (707); DP 1008; EP 1271; NP 1046

30. Thu. St. Jerome, P & D (Mem) 1275
     MP (1435) 824; DP 1012; EP (1436) 830; NP 1049

OCTOBER

1. Fri. St. Theresa of the Child Jesus, V & D (Mem) 1276
    MP (1435 or 1441) (Ant) 835; DP 1017; EP (1436 or 1444) (Ant) 840
    NP 1052

2. Sat. Guardian Angels (Mem) 1277
    MP 1277 (707); DP 1022; EP 851 (633); NP 1034

3. Sun. **TWENTY-SEVENTH SUNDAY IN ORDINARY TIME 633**
    MP 856; DP 994; EP 861; NP 1037

4. Mon. St. Francis of Assisi (Mem) 1283
    MP (1470) (Ant) 867; DP 998; EP (1471) (Ant) 872; NP 1041

5. Tue. Weekday or St. Faustina Kowalska, V *(New)* (1441 or 1470) or
       Bl. Francis Xavier Seelos, P *(New)* (1426)
    MP (1441 or 1470) (1426) 877; DP 1003
    EP (1444 or 1471) (1430) 882; NP 1044

6. Wed. Weekday or St. Bruno, P (1284) or Bl. Marie Rose Durocher, V
       (New) Pr proper (25)
    MP (1426 or 1470) (1441) 886; DP 1008
    EP (1430 or 1471) (1444) 892; NP 1046

7. Thu. Our Lady of the Rosary (Mem) 1284
    MP 1285 (707); DP 1012; EP 1286 (1378); NP 1049

8. Fri. Friday of the 27th Week in Ordinary Time
    MP 906; DP 1017; EP 911; NP 1052

9. Sat. Weekday or St. Denis, B & M, and Comps, Mm (1287) or St. John
       Leonardi, P (1288) or BVM on Saturday (1383)
    MP (1402) (1426 or 1472) (1383) 916; DP 1022; EP 921 (634); NP 1034

10. **Sun. TWENTY-EIGHTH SUNDAY IN ORDINARY TIME 634**
    MP 925; DP 994; EP 931; NP 1037

11. Mon. Weekday or St. John XXIII, Po *(New)* (1426)
    MP (1426) 937; DP 998; EP (1430) 942; NP 1041

12. Tue. Tuesday of the 28th Week in Ordinary Time
    MP 947; DP 1003; EP 953; NP 1044

13. Wed. Wednesday of the 28th Week in Ordinary Time
    MP 958; DP 1008; EP 963; NP 1046

14. Thu. Weekday or St. Callistus I, Po & M (1289)
    MP (1414 or 1426) 968; DP 1012; EP (1417 or 1430) 973; NP 1049

15. Fri. St. Teresa of Avila, V & D (Mem) 1289
    MP (1435 or 1441) 978; DP 1017; EP (1436 or 1444) 984; NP 1052

16. Sat. Weekday or St. Hedwig, Rel (1290) or St. Margaret Mary Alacoque,
    V (1290) or BVM on Saturday (1383)
    MP (1472 or 1470) (1441 or 1470) (1383) 988; DP 1022
    EP 701 (635); NP 1034

17. Sun. **TWENTY-NINTH SUNDAY IN ORDINARY TIME 635**
    MP 706; DP 994; EP 712; NP 1037

18. Mon. ST. LUKE, EVANGELIST (F) 1292
    MP 1293 (707); DP 998; EP 1295 (1394); NP 1041

19. Tue. Sts. Isaac Jogues and John de Brébeuf, Pp & Mm, and Comps,
    Mm (Mem) 1297
    MP (1402 or 1426) 728; DP 1003; EP (1405 or 1430) 734; NP 1044

20. Wed. Weekday or St. Paul of the Cross, P (1297) **[transferred from
    10/19]**
    MP (1426) 738; DP 1008; EP (1430) 743; NP 1046

21. Thu. Thursday of the 29th Week in Ordinary Time
    MP 748; DP 1012; EP 754; NP 1049

22. Fri. Weekday or St. John Paul II, Po *(New)* (1426)
    MP (1426) 759; DP 1017; EP (1430) 765; NP 1052

23. Sat. Weekday or St. John of Capistrano, P (1298) or BVM on Saturday
    (1383)
    MP (1426) (1383) 770; DP 1022; EP (636) 775; NP 1034

24. Sun. **THIRTIETH SUNDAY IN ORDINARY TIME 636**
    MP 780; DP 994; EP 786; NP 1037

25. Mon. Monday of the 30th Week in Ordinary Time
    MP 793; DP 998; EP 798; NP 1041

26. Tue. Tuesday of the 30th Week in Ordinary Time
    MP 802; DP 1003; EP 807; NP 1044

27. Wed. Wednesday of the 30th Week in Ordinary Time
    MP 812; DP 1008; EP 818; NP 1046

28. Thu. STS. SIMON AND JUDE, AP (F) 1299
    MP 1392 (707); DP 1012; EP 1394; NP 1049

29. Fri. Friday of the 30th Week in Ordinary Time
    MP 835; DP 1017; EP 840; NP 1052

30. Sat. Weekday or BVM on Saturday (1383)
    MP (1383) 845; DP 1022; EP (637) 851; NP 1034

31. Sun. **THIRTY-FIRST SUNDAY IN ORDINARY TIME 637**
    MP 856; DP 994; EP 1300; NP 1034

NOVEMBER

1. Mon. **ALL SAINTS (Sol) 1304**
   MP 1304 (707); DP 1027; EP 1306; NP 1037

2. Tue. ALL SOULS 1310
   MP 1486; DP 1493; EP 1497; NP 1037

3. Wed. Weekday or St. Martin de Porres, Rel (1310)
    MP (1470) (Ant) 886; DP 1008; EP (1471) (Ant) 892; NP 1046

4. Thu. St. Charles Borromeo, B (Mem) 1311
    MP (1426) 897; DP 1012; EP (1430) 901; NP 1049

5. Fri. Friday of the 31st Week in Ordinary Time
    MP 906; DP 1017; EP 911; NP 1052

6. Sat. Weekday or BVM on Saturday (1383)
    MP (1383) 916; DP 1022; EP (638) 921;NP 1034

7. Sun. **THIRTY-SECOND SUNDAY IN ORDINARY TIME 638**
    MP 925; DP 994; EP 931; NP 1037

8. Mon. Monday of the 32nd Week in Ordinary Time
    MP 937; DP 998; EP 942; NP 1041

9. Tue. DEDICATION OF SAINT JOHN LATERAN (F) 1312
    MP 1360 (707); DP 1003; EP 1363; NP 1044

10. Wed. St. Leo the Great, Po & D (Mem) 1312
    MP (1426 or 1435) (Ant) 958; DP 1008
    EP (1430 or 1436) (Ant) 963; NP 1046

11. Thu. St. Martin of Tours, B (Mem) 1313
    MP 1314 (707); DP 1012; EP 1315 (1430); NP 1049

12. Fri. St. Josaphat, B & M (Mem) 1316
    MP (1414 or 1426) 978; DP 1017
    EP (1417 or 1430) 984; NP 1052

13. Sat. St. Frances Xavier Cabrini, V (Mem) 1317
    MP (1441 or 1470 or 1472) 988; DP 1022
    EP (639) 701; NP 1034

14. **Sun. THIRTY-THIRD SUNDAY IN ORDINARY TIME 639**
     MP 706; DP 994; EP 712; NP 1037

15. Mon. Weekday or St. Albert, B & D (1318)
     MP (1426 or 1435) 718; DP 998; EP (1430 or 1436) 723; NP 1041

16. Tue. Weekday or St. Margaret of Scotland (1319) or St. Gertrude, V
         (1319)
     MP (1472) (1441 or 1470) 728; DP 1003
     EP (1472) (1444 or 1471) 734; NP 1044

17. Wed. St. Elizabeth of Hungary (Mem) 1320
     MP (1472) 738; DP 1008; EP (1472) 743; NP 1046

18. Thu. Weekday or Dedication of the Churches of Sts. Peter and Paul, Ap
         (1321) or St. Rose Philippine Duchesne, V **(New)** (26)
     MP (1392) (1441) (Ant) 748; DP 1012
     EP (1394) (1444) (Ant) 754; NP 1049

19. Fri. Friday of the 33rd Week in Ordinary Time
     MP 759; DP 1017; EP 765; NP 1052

20. Sat. Weekday or BVM on Saturday (1383)
     MP (1383) 770; DP 1022; EP (674) 775; NP 1034

21. **Sun. CHRIST THE KING (Sol) 677**
     MP 677 (707); DP 1027; EP 679; NP 1037

22. Mon. St. Cecilia, V & M (Mem) 1323
     MP (1414 or 1441) (Ant) 792; DP 998
     EP (1417 or 1444) (Ant) 798; NP 1041

23. Tue. Weekday or St. Clement I, Po & M (1324) or St. Columban, Ab
         (1324) or Bl. Miguel Agustín Pro, P & M **(New)** (27)

MP (1414 or 1426) (1426 or 1470) 802; DP 1003
EP (1417 or 1430) (1430 or 1471) 807; NP 1044

24. Wed. St. Andrew Dung-Lac, P, and Comps, Mm (Mem) **(New)** (28)
MP (1402) 812; DP 1008; EP (1405) 818; NP 1046

25. Thu. Weekday or St. Catherine of Alexandria, V & M *(New)* (1414 or 1441)
MP (1414 or 1441) 824; DP 1012; EP (1417 or 1444) 830; NP 1049

26. Fri. Friday of the 34th Week in Ordinary Time
MP 835; DP 1017; EP 840; NP 1052

27. Sat. Weekday or BVM on Saturday (1383)
MP (1383) 845; DP 1022; EP (41) 701; NP 1034

28. **Sun. FIRST SUNDAY OF ADVENT 43**
MP (43) 706; DP 994; EP (45) 712; NP 1037

29. Mon. Monday of the 1st Week of Advent
MP (47) 718; DP 998; EP (48) 723; NP 1041

30. Tue. ST. ANDREW, AP (F) 1325
MP 1325 (707); DP 1003; EP 1327 (1394); NP 1044

DECEMBER

1. Wed. Wednesday of the 1st Week of Advent
MP (53) 738; DP 1008; EP (54) 743; NP 1046

2. Thu. Thursday of the 1st Week of Advent
MP (56) 748; DP 1012; EP (57) 754; NP 1049

3. Fri. St. Francis Xavier, P (Mem) 1329
   MP (1426) 759; DP 1017; EP (1430) 765; NP 1052

4. Sat. Advent Weekday or St. John Damascene, P & D (1330)
   MP (1435) (62) 770; DP 1022; EP (64) 775; NP 1034

5. **Sun. SECOND SUNDAY OF ADVENT 66**
   MP (66) 780; DP 994; EP (68) 786; NP 1037

6. Mon. Advent Weekday or St. Nicholas, B (1330)
   MP (1426) (70) 792; DP 998; EP (1430) (72) 798; NP 1041

7. Tue. St. Ambrose, B & D (Mem) 1331
   MP (1435) 802; DP 1003; EP 1332 (1368); NP 1034

8. **Wed. IMMACULATE CONCEPTION (Sol) 1334**
   MP 1334 (707); DP 1027; EP 1336 (1378); NP 1037

9. Thu. Advent Weekday or St. Juan Diego **(New)** (32)
   MP (1452) (79) 824; DP 1012
   EP (1455) (80) 830; NP 1049

10. Fri. Friday of the 2nd Week of Advent
    MP (82) 835; DP 1017; EP (83) 840; NP 1052

11. Sat. Advent Weekday or St. Damasus I, Po (1339)
    MP (1426) (85) 845; DP 1022; EP (87) 851; NP 1034

12. **Sun. THIRD SUNDAY OF ADVENT 89**
    MP (89) 856; DP 994; EP (91) 861; NP 1037

13. Mon. St. Lucy, V & M (Mem) 1341
    MP (1414 or 1441) (Ant) 867; DP 998
    EP (1417 or 1444) (Ant) 872; NP 1041

14.   Tue. St. John of the Cross, P & D (Mem) 1342
    MP (1435) 877; DP 1003; EP (1436) 882; NP 1044

15.   Wed. Wednesday of the 3rd Week of Advent
    MP (100) 886; DP 1008; EP (102) 892; NP 1046

16.   Thu. Thursday of the 3rd Week of Advent
    MP (103) 897; DP 1012; EP (105) 901; NP 1049

17.   Fri. Friday of the 3rd Week of Advent
    MP (116) 906; DP 1017; EP (117) 911; NP 1052

18.   Sat. Saturday of the 3rd Week of Advent
    MP (119) 916; DP 1022; EP (110) 921; NP 1034

19.   **Sun. FOURTH SUNDAY OF ADVENT 111**
    MP (112) 926 (Ant 122); DP 994; EP (114) 931 (Ant 124); NP 1037

20.   Mon. Monday of the 4th Week of Advent
    MP (125) 937; DP 998; EP (126) 942; NP 1041

21.   Tue. Tuesday of the 4th Week of Advent
    MP (128) 947 (St. Peter Canisius 1343); DP 1003
    EP (129) 953 (St. Peter Canisius 1343); NP 1044

22.   Wed. Wednesday of the 4th Week of Advent
    MP (131) 958; DP 1008; EP (132) 963; NP 1046

23.   Thu. Thursday of the 4th Week of Advent
    MP (134) 968 (St. John of Kanty 1344); DP 1012
    EP (136) 973 (St. John of Kanty 1344); NP 1049

24.   Fri. Friday of the 4th Week of Advent
    MP (137) 978; DP 1017; EP 140; NP 1034

25. **Sat. CHRISTMAS (Sol) 144**
     MP 144 (707); DP 1027; EP 147; NP 1034 or 1037

26. **Sun. HOLY FAMILY (F) 154**
     MP 154 (707); DP 994; EP 156 (1378); NP 1034 or 1037

27. Mon. ST. JOHN, AP & EVANGELIST (F) 1347
     MP 1347 (707); DP 998; EP 147 & 161; NP 1034 or 1037

28. Tue. HOLY INNOCENTS, MM (F) 1349
     MP 1349 (707); DP 1003; EP 147 & 162; NP 1034 or 1037

29. Wed. FIFTH DAY IN THE OCTAVE OF CHRISTMAS
     MP 144 & 164 (St. Thomas Becket, B & M 1352); DP 1008
     EP 147 & 165 (St. Thomas Becket, B & M 1352); NP 1034 or 1037

30. Thu. SIXTH DAY IN THE OCTAVE OF CHRISTMAS
     MP 144 & 168; DP 1012; EP 147 & 169; NP 1034 or 1037

31. Fri. SEVENTH DAY IN THE OCTAVE OF CHRISTMAS
     MP 144 & 171 (St. Sylvester I, Po 1353); DP 1017
     EP 173 (1368); NP 1034 or 1037

Prayer

(For use on May 24, The Blessed Virgin Mary, Mother of the Church [Memorial])

O God, Father of mercies,
whose Only Begotten Son, as he hung upon the Cross,
chose the Blessed Virgin Mary, his Mother,
to be our Mother also,
grant, we pray, that with her loving help
your Church may be more fruitful day by day
and, exulting in the holiness of her children,
may draw to her embrace all the families of the peoples.
Through our Lord Jesus Christ, your Son,
who lives and reigns with you in the unity of the Holy Spirit,
one God, for ever and ever.

CHRISTIAN PRAYER

This regular-size edition of the official one-volume edition of the internationally acclaimed Liturgy of the Hours contains the complete texts of Morning and Evening Prayer for the entire year. With its readable 10-pt. type, ribbon markers for easy location of texts, and beautiful two-color printing, this handy volume simplifies praying the official Prayer of the Church for today's busy Catholic.

No. 406/19—Dura-Lux Binding **$44.00**
ISBN 978-1-941243-61-9

SHORTER CHRISTIAN PRAYER

This abbreviated version of the internationally acclaimed Liturgy of the Hours contains Morning and Evening Prayer from the Four-Week Psalter and selected texts for the Seasons and Major Feasts of the year. Printed in two colors, this volume includes a useful ribbon marker. Its handy, practical size makes this edition ideal for parish use.

No. 408/19—Dura-Lux Binding **$21.00**
ISBN 978-1-941243-60-2

LITURGY OF THE HOURS

This is the official English edition of the Divine Office that contains the translation approved by the International Commission on English in the Liturgy.

709/13

No. 409/10 Set of 4 volumes............................... **$159.00**
ISBN 978-0-89942-409-5

No. 409/13 Set of 4 volumes—Black Leather Binding
Note: available in sets only.................................. **$181.00**
ISBN 978-0-89942-411-8

No. 709/13 Set of 4 volumes—Large Print, Leather Binding. *Note: available in sets only*................... **$199.00**
ISBN 978-0-89942-710-2

ACTUAL SIZE TYPE

READING

I know well the plans I have Lord, plans for your welfare, n you a future full of hope. When

409/10

409/13

41

A Companion to the Liturgy of the Hours: Morning and Evening Prayer

By Shirley Darcus Sullivan

A spiritual companion for Morning and Evening Prayer of the Four-Week Psalter. It presents ways in which the experience of the Hours may be made more prayerful for those who say them, e.g., by using the spirituality of Carmel, especially that of Elizabeth of the Trinity. 208 pages. Size 5½ x 8¼. Flexible full-color paper cover.

No. 415/04
ISBN: 978-0-89942-432-3
Price: $9.95

The Divine Office for Dodos

A Step-by-Step Guide to Praying the Liturgy of the Hours

By Madeline Pecora Nugent

For those who want to pray all the Hours correctly and completely, this book contains over 90 detailed lessons with questions, helpful hints, and practice sessions presented in a simple style. 272 pages. Size $5^{1}/_{4}$ x $7^{3}/_{4}$.

"There is hope in these pages! You are going to learn to pray the Divine Office! Honest! Then you will join the ranks of other clergy, religious, and laity, some of whom are non-Catholic, who pray the Divine Office every day."—From the Author's Introduction

No. 416/04
ISBN: 978-0-89942-482-8
Price: $8.95

PRACTICAL GUIDE FOR THE LITURGY OF THE HOURS

PRACTICAL GUIDE FOR THE LITURGY OF THE HOURS—By Shirley Sullivan. This book begins with a treatment of the two main Hours of Morning and Evening Prayer and then also presents the other Hours. It offers guidance to individuals as well as for groups to pray in a rich and meaningful way. 96 pages. Size $4^3/_8$ x $6^3/_4$.

No. 426/04—Flexible cover ISBN 978-0-89942-484-2 . . . .**$5.95**

COMPANION PRAYER BOOK TO THE LITURGY OF THE HOURS

COMPANION PRAYER BOOK TO THE LITURGY OF THE HOURS—By Georges-Albert Boissinot. This book is meant to help all clergy, religious, and lay people to share more fully in the Prayer of the Church through inspirational prayers and reflections centered on the celebration of the Hours. 128 pages. Size $4^3/_8$ x $6^3/_4$.

No. 434/04—Flexible cover ISBN 978-0-89942-354-8 . . . .**$7.95**

OTHER OUTSTANDING CATHOLIC BOOKS

HOLY BIBLE—The Saint Joseph Edition of the **NEW CATHOLIC BIBLE (NCB)** is a fresh, faithful, and reader-friendly translation. All editions are intended to be used by Catholics for daily prayer and meditation, as well as private devotion and group study. The editions feature Large, Readable Type, Rich Explanatory Notes, Maps, Photographs, a section entitled "Learning about Your Bible," and a Doctrinal Bible Index.

Family Edition	**No. 614**
Giant Type Edition	**No. 617**

NEW TESTAMENT—St. Joseph Edition of the **NEW CATHOLIC BIBLE** translation. Large, easy-to-read type, with helpful Notes and Maps. Features the words of Christ in red.

Vest Pocket Edition	**No. 650**
Study Edition—Includes many helps.	**No. 311**
Pocket Edition—Illustrated. (Christ's words not in red.)	**No. 630**

THE PSALMS—St. Joseph **NEW CATHOLIC BIBLE,** printed in large, easy-to-read type with copious informative notes and cross-references.

	No. 665

New St. Joseph
Handbook for Lectors & Proclaimers of the Word
Liturgical Year B — 2021
Rev. Jude Winkler, OFM Conv.

Unique and Valuable Features of This Catholic Book Publishing Edition:

✔ Contains the approved New American Bible text of the Readings for Sunday Mass (including Holy Thursday, Good Friday, and the Easter Vigil) for 2021.

✔ Helpful Commentary guides the lector or proclaimer of the Word to understand the context and background of the reading being proclaimed.

✔ Full text for each Mass, including the Responsorial Psalm and Alleluia Verse.

✔ Attractive Format—Each page has been very carefully arranged with optimum leading between lines and extra space between Readings.

✔ Magnificently Illustrated—Over 60 liturgical drawings enhance the beauty of this text.

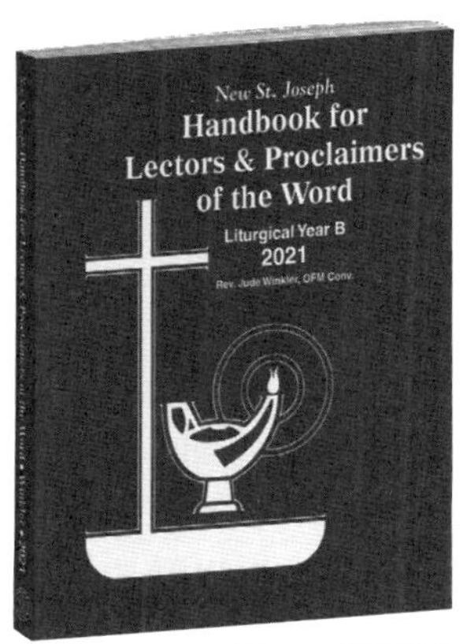

No. 85/04
ISBN 978-0-89942-086-8
Price: $10.95

✔ Clear Running Heads show at a glance the date and title of every Sunday reading.

✔ Complete Text included for both longer and shorter forms of readings.

✔ Handy Index of Bible Texts enables lector or proclaimer to locate at a glance every Reading, Responsorial Psalm, or Alleluia Verse or Verse before the Gospel used during the current year.

✔ Helpful Short Glossary and Complete Pronunciation Guide.

✔ Large size: 8 1/2 x 11.

✔ Durable Binding.

✔ Excellent Resource for R.C.I.A. Study Groups.

OTHER OUTSTANDING CATHOLIC BOOKS

St. Joseph SUNDAY MISSAL—Complete Edition . . . in accord with *The Roman Misssal*, Third Edition. Includes all 3 Cycles (**A, B, and C**) with explanations. 1,600 pages. **No. 820**

St. Joseph WEEKDAY MISSAL (Vol. I & II)—All the Mass texts needed for weekdays in accord with *The Roman Misssal*, Third Edition. An indispensable aid for all who celebrate and participate at daily Mass. **Nos. 920 & 921**
Large Type Edition **Nos. 922 & 923**

St. Joseph SUNDAY MISSAL—LARGE TYPE EDITION—Includes the Readings for the 3-year Cycle printed in extra-large type for easy reading. Includes full-color inserts. **No. 822**

St. Joseph CHURCH HISTORY—Sets forth the major events in the life of the Church in a clear and logical fashion that makes them understandable to the modern reader. Large type. Illustrated. **No. 262**

BIBLE MEDITATIONS FOR EVERY DAY—By Rev. John C. Kersten, S.V.D. Excellent aid for daily meditation. A Scripture passage and a short, invaluable introduction are given for every day. **No. 277**

MARY DAY BY DAY—Introduction by Rev. Charles G. Fehrenbach, C.SS.R. Minute Marian meditations for every day of the year, including a Scripture passage, a quotation from the Saints, and a concluding prayer. Over 300 illustrations in two colors. **No. 180**

NEW SAINT JOSEPH PEOPLE'S PRAYER BOOK—Edited by Rev. Francis Evans. An encyclopedia of prayers, drawn from the Bible and Liturgy, the *Enchiridion of Indulgences*, the Saints and spiritual writers—plus hundreds of traditional and contemporary prayers for every need. Over 1,400 prayers typeset in sense lines. Large type. Printed and illustrated in two colors. 1,056 pages. **No. 900**

FOLLOWING THE HOLY SPIRIT—By Rev. Walter van de Putte, C.S.Sp. Patterned after **The Imitation of Christ,** it contains dialogues with, and prayers to, the Holy Spirit. Large type. Illustrated. **No. 335**

MARY MY HOPE—By Rev. Lawrence G. Lovasik, S.V.D. Popular book of devotions to Mary. Large type. Illustrated. **No. 365**

OTHER OUTSTANDING CATHOLIC BOOKS

TREASURY OF NOVENAS—By Rev. Lawrence G. Lovasik, S.V.D. More than forty popular Novenas carefully arranged for private prayer in accord with the Liturgical Year on the Feasts of Jesus, Mary, and favorite Saints. With full-color inserts.   **No. 345**

DAILY REFLECTIONS WITH MARY—By Rev. Rawley Myers. A beautifully illustrated and printed book that gives thirty-one prayerful Marian reflections plus a large selection of prayers to Our Lady. Every page is written out of deep love for Mary and inculcates a great devotion to her.   **No. 372**

THE IMITATION OF CHRIST—By Thomas à Kempis. The one book that is second only to the Bible in popularity. Large type. Illustrated.   **No. 320**

THE IMITATION OF MARY—By Rev. Alexander de Rouville, S.J. Companion volume to **The Imitation of Christ.** Large type. Illustrated.   **No. 330**

LIVES OF THE SAINTS—Short life of a Saint and prayer for every day of the year. Over 50 illustrations. Ideal for daily meditation and private study.   **No. 870**

PRAYERS FOR ALL OCCASIONS—By Rev. Francis Evans. Inspiring prayer book with a wealth of timely prayers for any occasion. Large type. Printed in two colors.   **No. 917**

PRAYERS FOR URGENT OCCASIONS—By Bernard Marie, O.F.S. Beautiful prayer book containing the prayers and devotions that will be of help in times of trial. Printed in two colors.   **No. 918**

FAVORITE PRAYERS TO OUR LADY—By Anthony M. Buono. Contains prayers to Mary under her titles, for Novenas and devotions, for various occasions, for liturgical seasons, and for every month and each day of the week. Printed in full color.   **No. 919**

CATHOLIC TREASURY OF PRAYERS—A prayer companion for all time. Features sections devoted to the Mass, the Psalms, and prayers to Our Blessed Mother, St. Joseph, and Patron Saints.   **No. 938**

catholicbookpublishing.com

The
LITURGY OF THE HOURS
is truly the prayer of the Church
for all the people of God —
bishops, priests, deacons,
religious and the
laity.

ISBN 978-1-953152-04-6

This Guide is No. 407/G
ISBN 978-1-953152-04-6